Original title:
Wings of Ambition

Copyright © 2025 Swan Charm
All rights reserved.

Author: Liisi Lendorav
ISBN HARDBACK: 978-9908-1-4825-0
ISBN PAPERBACK: 978-9908-1-4826-7
ISBN EBOOK: 978-9908-1-4827-4

Glide on the Air of Possibilities

Wings spread wide in morning light,
Dreams take off, a wondrous flight.
Clouds beneath, a soft embrace,
Infinite paths, no time to waste.

With every breeze, new chances call,
Lifted high, we fear not fall.
Horizons stretch, a beckoning sea,
In this space, we learn to be.

The Soarer's Journey

Through valleys deep and mountains tall,
A spirit bold, ready to crawl.
Each step counts, the sky so clear,
A heart unbound, with nothing to fear.

The sun will rise, guiding the way,
In the twilight, dreams softly sway.
With wings of hope, soaring supreme,
Chasing whispers of each bright dream.

Ascendant Visions

A prism of colors, visions ignite,
In every shadow, we find our light.
Ascent begins with a single thought,
In realms of wonder, battles fought.

Each heartbeat echoes, a rhythmic dance,
In fragile stillness, we take a chance.
The canvas spreads, vast and free,
Each stroke a promise of what could be.

The Echo of Longing Paths

Footsteps linger on the ground,
Whispers of dreams, a haunting sound.
In every turn, a tale to weave,
In memories held, we learn to believe.

With every echo, a journey calls,
Through shadowed halls, where longing falls.
We seek the stars, a guiding light,
In woven fates, we find our flight.

Soaring Dreams

In the quiet dawn, hopes ignite,
Whispers of wishes take to flight.
Above the clouds, where eagles roam,
Hearts find strength in their skyward home.

Stars guide the way, a shimmering path,
Through trials and storms, we find our wrath.
With wings of faith, we chase the sun,
Embracing the journey, it's just begun.

Beneath the Feathered Horizon

Beneath a sky of endless blue,
Where dreams take shape and hearts renew.
Feathered wings in graceful dance,
Weaving a tale of sweet romance.

With every breeze, we lift and glide,
Over valleys wide, on hope we ride.
The sun dips low; colors ablaze,
In the twilight glow, our spirits raise.

Climbing the Heights of Desire

Upward we strive, with fervor bold,
In mountains steep, where dreams unfold.
With every step, the summit calls,
Echoes of wishes through canyon walls.

The air grows thin, yet we push through,
With hearts ablaze and spirits true.
At the peak, the world sprawls wide,
In the heights of desire, we abide.

Flight of the Aspiring Soul

A soul takes wing, in search of light,
Through shadows cast, it yearns for flight.
With every heartbeat, a dream takes shape,
In the fabric of stars, a grand escape.

The winds of change, they softly call,
In the dance of life, we rise, we fall.
Yet through it all, we find our way,
On the flight of dreams, we choose to stay.

The Ascendancy Whisper

In shadows deep where silence dwells,
A whisper stirs, the heart compels.
Hope flickers like a distant star,
Guiding dreams both near and far.

Through trials faced and struggles tall,
We rise together, never fall.
The winds of change, a gentle guide,
In unity, our fears subside.

A spark ignites within the soul,
With every step, we reach our goal.
The climb is steep, but hands entwined,
We find the strength, our dreams aligned.

Through valleys low and mountains high,
We lift our gaze and touch the sky.
The dawn awakens, hope anew,
In whispered tones, our hearts break through.

Together bound by dreams we weave,
In ascent, we find the courage to believe.
With every challenge, every fight,
We chase the dawn, embrace the light.

On Gossamer Dreams

In twilight's glow, soft wishes glide,
On silver threads, our hopes reside.
Each breath a promise, bright and clear,
In gossamer dreams, we hold what's dear.

A dance of stars in velvet skies,
Where every wish begins to rise.
We spin our tales on moonlit beams,
As night unfolds, we chase our dreams.

With fragile hearts, we dare to soar,
Past earthly bounds, to distant shores.
In every heartbeat, echoes affirm,
Gossamer dreams ignite the firm.

Through storms that rage and wild winds blow,
We find our wings, we learn to flow.
In whispered secrets, truths untold,
On gossamer dreams, our hopes unfold.

Together we tread on paths unknown,
With every step, our spirits grown.
In the tapestry of life, we gleam,
Forever bound in gossamer dreams.

The Skies We Dare to Conquer

Beneath the vast, uncharted blue,
We set our sights, our dreams in view.
With hearts ablaze, we face the day,
The skies await, we'll find our way.

Through clouds of doubt and storms that rage,
We break the bounds, we turn the page.
With every breath, we take to flight,
Into the dawn, we chase the light.

Each star above, a dream ignites,
Guiding us through the darkest nights.
With courage fierce, we navigate,
The skies we dare, we will create.

From every struggle, strength we gain,
With every triumph, joy remains.
Together braving every storm,
In conquering skies, our hearts grow warm.

With wings of hope, we soar so high,
To touch the dreams that fill the sky.
In unity, our spirits sing,
The skies we dare to conquer bring.

Rising Tides of Aspiration

From distant shores, a tide does swell,
With whispers soft, our dreams compel.
The waves of change, they crash and roll,
In rising tides, we seek our goal.

Through currents strong, we forge ahead,
With every step, our spirit fed.
The horizon calls, a beacon bright,
In rising tides, we chase the light.

With every challenge, every fear,
We stand as one, our vision clear.
In unity, we find our way,
Through rising tides, we'll seize the day.

Embracing change, we learn to grow,
With hearts on fire, we'll steal the show.
For in the depths, our dreams reside,
In rising tides of aspiration, we glide.

Together we ride the waves of fate,
With courage fierce, we create our state.
In every heartbeat, we ignite,
The rising tides of dreams take flight.

Soaring Dreams

In the quiet of the night,
Stars whisper, taking flight.
Weaving wishes, hearts ignite,
Soaring dreams, a soul's delight.

Through the dark, a path is shown,
With the courage we have grown.
Hands reach high, seeds of hope sown,
Boundless skies, we're not alone.

Clouds may gather, storms may roar,
But we rise, forever more.
In the winds, our spirits soar,
Chasing dreams and tales of yore.

On the wings of bright ideals,
With every heartbeat, fervor feels.
A journey thrives in shared appeals,
Together, lifted, joy reveals.

Trust the call, let instincts guide,
In unity, hearts abide.
To these dreams, we will not hide,
With each breath, our worlds collide.

Boundless Horizons

Beyond the hills where shadows play,
A brighter dawn greets the day.
Horizons stretch, in colors sway,
Boundless skies, a grand ballet.

Carved in light, the paths unveil,
Stories whispered on the gale.
Through every trial, we prevail,
Chasing futures without fail.

Mountains rise, the challenges, stark,
Yet, we kindle every spark.
In our hearts, we make a mark,
Finding strength in every arc.

With every step, the world expands,
United by these hopeful strands.
Together, chasing distant lands,
Embracing fate with open hands.

So dream aloud, let visions fly,
For boundless joys will never die.
In the echoes, we comply,
Endless futures in the sky.

Flight of the Aspirants

In the dawn, aspirations glow,
Setting sails on winds that blow.
Hearts alight with fervent flow,
In this flight, we come to know.

With each challenge, we will bend,
But like rivers, we transcend.
Courage found in every friend,
On this journey, hopes defend.

Take the leap, embrace the change,
The vast unknown may feel strange.
Yet with trust, we can arrange,
Dreams and destinies exchange.

Through the skies, our spirits rise,
Painted wings, we mesmerize.
In the currents, truths disguise,
Sailing high where freedom lies.

Together we'll stake our claim,
In this quest, we'll stake our name.
Through the storms, we'll fan the flame,
Flight of aspirants, our aim.

Rise Above the Clouds

When the night seeks to confine,
With our dreams, we draw the line.
Hearts united, spirits shine,
Together, we will intertwine.

Amidst the gray, we seek the blue,
With each heartbeat, strong and true.
A dawn awaits, refreshing view,
Rising high, we start anew.

Above the clouds, our spirits soar,
In harmony, forever more.
With every heartbeat, we explore,
A boundless world, an open door.

Venturing where few have tread,
With every step, we're gently led.
Hope ignites where fears have fled,
In the light, our dreams are fed.

So let us rise, let burdens fall,
In each other, we stand tall.
With every breath, we heed the call,
Above the clouds, we'll have it all.

The Journey of Yearning

In shadows deep, the heart will roam,
Seeking solace, far from home.
Each step a whisper, a silent creed,
To find the place where dreams take seed.

Paths are winding, the way unsure,
Yet hope ignites like a burning lure.
With every turn, a lesson learned,
For every page, the heart has yearned.

Mountains rise, and valleys call,
In every stumble, we find our thrall.
With every tear, a strength will grow,
To chase the light, to let love flow.

Through storms we wander, in sun, we bask,
To seek the answers, a fervent task.
The journey leads us far and wide,
In every moment, our souls abide.

When finally we reach the dawn,
We'll look back at the paths we've drawn.
For in the yearning, we've grown wise,
To embrace the journey, the ultimate prize.

Dreams on the Breeze

Whispers of dreams ride the air,
Dancing lightly without a care.
Each thought a feather, soft and bright,
Carried aloft in the moon's soft light.

In fields of stars, our wishes soar,
Painting the night with what we adore.
With eyes wide open, we chase the gleam,
Sailing softly on the wings of a dream.

Gentle winds weave through our souls,
Collecting hopes, as the music rolls.
In every heartbeat, a wish takes flight,
Cradled gently in the arms of night.

Clouds of wonder drift above,
Whispers of destiny, wrapped in love.
A symphony of laughter fills the space,
As we surrender to time and grace.

Let the dreams guide us, ever high,
Boundless horizons, as we fly.
With every breath, we find our ease,
In a world alive with dreams on the breeze.

A Skyward Quest

Beneath the heavens, our spirits climb,
In the vast expanse, we lose all time.
Stars our compass, bright and clear,
Guiding us on, year after year.

With open hearts, we chase the glow,
In endless skies, our passions flow.
Each challenge faced, a seed is sown,
In every moment, we carve our throne.

Clouds may gather, the storms may rise,
Yet through the darkness, we find our skies.
With courage fierce, we push ahead,
In the quest for dreams that dance like threads.

Through valleys deep and mountains tall,
We gather wisdom, we hear the call.
With every trial, our spirits grow,
Fueling the fire that we bestow.

Ascend the heights, let fear release,
In unity, we find our peace.
Together we soar, our hearts aligned,
In the skyward quest, true freedom we find.

Ascend the Heights

In the dawn's light, we climb anew,
With every fiber, our spirits true.
Each step a promise, a vow we make,
To seek the summit, for our own sake.

The world below fades into dreams,
As we ascend, or so it seems.
Each heart that beats, a rhythm grand,
Together we rise, hand in hand.

The air grows thin, yet we press on,
Fueled by hope, until the stars are gone.
With every struggle, a fire ignites,
To conquer the peaks of our heart's delights.

From rocky ledges to skies so blue,
In this ascent, we find the true.
With every glance back at the trail behind,
We realize the treasures we've defined.

As we stand tall and touch the sky,
In the heights we've climbed, we learn to fly.
With open hearts and spirits bright,
We celebrate the journey, the endless light.

Embracing the Vastness Above

In the quiet of the night,
Stars shimmer, oh so bright.
Whispers float on gentle air,
In their glow, we lose our care.

Clouds drift softly, dreams awake,
In their arms, our hearts shall take.
Above us, worlds we long to know,
Guided by the moon's faint glow.

Each moment filled with wonder,
As we gaze in awe, we ponder.
Empty skies paint tales untold,
Stories of the brave and bold.

Mountains rise like ancient guards,
In their shadows, life rewards.
Embrace the vastness, take a flight,
Into the depths of endless night.

With every star, a path ignites,
Leading souls to lofty heights.
In the quiet we reflect,
The vastness calls, we intersect.

The Call of Daring Heights

Lifting eyes to azure skies,
We hear the call, we feel it rise.
Hearts aflame with dreams untamed,
Each step forward, bold and aimed.

Through the peaks, the winds sing clear,
With every challenge, we adhere.
The summit beckons, strong and true,
A world awaits for me and you.

With climbing boots and spirits high,
We chase the sunsets, let us fly.
Each rock a story, every crest,
A testament to questing zest.

Whispers from the heights we chase,
In the clouds, we find our place.
A daring spirit, call so bright,
Together, we conquer, take our flight.

As shadows stretch and sunlight fades,
We dance in dreams, our fears cascade.
On daring heights, we stand so tall,
In the embrace of nature's call.

Hearts Unchained

In a world of fleeting time,
We find the rhythm, hearts in rhyme.
Boundless dreams, we fly so high,
No more limits, we touch the sky.

Hand in hand, through storms we tread,
No more shadows, no more dread.
Love unshackled, free to roam,
In each other, we find our home.

With every heartbeat, whispers flow,
In each glance, the embers grow.
Together, we rewrite our fate,
Two wild souls refuse to wait.

Through every trial, love remains,
In the fire, we've shed the chains.
Our spirits dance, no longer pain,
In this journey, hearts unchained.

With open arms, we greet the dawn,
A canvas fresh, no need to yawn.
Hearts ablaze, forever true,
In our bond, we start anew.

The Pursuit of Celestial Light

Chasing dreams through starry nights,
We seek the glow of ancient lights.
Fleeting shadows in our wake,
We follow paths that silence makes.

With every step, the cosmos calls,
A serenade that softly falls.
Through swirling fields of stardust bright,
We dance beneath the cosmic height.

In whispered tones, the universe speaks,
To wandering hearts, to daring peaks.
We run with joy, we leap with grace,
In this pursuit, we find our place.

Radiant beams illuminate the dark,
Igniting hope with every spark.
The vastness holds our dreams so tight,
In the quest for celestial light.

Together, we reach for the divine,
In each heartbeat, our souls entwine.
As we wander through endless nights,
We embrace the beauty of divine sights.

Circling the Sun of Possibility

In the dawn's golden light, we rise,
Chasing dreams that paint the skies.
Hope flickers like a distant star,
Guiding us to who we are.

With each step, the world unfolds,
Stories waiting to be told.
Beyond the horizon, hearts ignite,
In the warmth of possibilities bright.

Whispers of courage fill the air,
Embracing moments, wild and rare.
We dance on paths both new and old,
In the sun's embrace, we break the mold.

A tapestry of dreams we weave,
In every heart, the urge to believe.
Circling around our hopes so free,
Together in this endless spree.

In the end, it's not the chase,
But the journey, the joy we face.
Under the sun, we find our way,
In the light of possibility's play.

From Shadows to Skylines

In shadows deep, where silence dwells,
A whisper speaks, a story tells.
Beneath the weight of doubt and fear,
Hope rises up, its voice sincere.

Each step we take from dark to light,
Transforms the world, ignites the night.
With courage as our guiding star,
We reach for dreams that feel afar.

Skylines shimmer with promise bright,
As we emerge, hearts taking flight.
From shadows long, we break the chains,
Embracing joy amid the pains.

With every glance, the past we shed,
A canvas wide where dreams are bred.
Together we ignite the flame,
In unity, we rise, reclaim.

From shadows past to future's grace,
We carve our path, we find our place.
Through trials faced, we now ascend,
In the skyline's glow, our spirits blend.

A Canvas of Aspirations

Upon a canvas, blank and wide,
Colors swirl and dreams abide.
Each brushstroke tells a tale anew,
Of hopes and visions breaking through.

With vibrant hues, we paint our fate,
Lines of courage, love, and hate.
In every shade, our voices rise,
Creating worlds beneath the skies.

The whispers of our hearts combine,
Creating art that's truly mine.
From deepest blues to fiery reds,
The stories of our lives spread.

In every corner, light may gleam,
We shape our goals, we craft our dream.
A masterpiece of sheer delight,
A canvas of aspirations bright.

As days go by, the colors change,
New paths reveal, new dreams exchange.
In this artwork, we find our role,
With every stroke, we free our soul.

The Lift of Unshackled Souls

In chains no more, we take our flight,
Soaring high into the light.
Unshackled souls, we rise and roam,
Finding solace in the unknown.

With wings of freedom, hearts ablaze,
We chase the dawn, embrace the maze.
Through valleys low and mountains high,
The spirit dances, learns to fly.

In laughter loud and silence deep,
Our voices blend, our dreams we keep.
Across the skies, the echoes call,
Together we rise, never to fall.

With every breath, we claim our place,
In the world's vast, embracing space.
The lift we feel, a boundless goal,
A testament to the unshackled soul.

In unity, we find our strength,
A tapestry of life at length.
For in this journey of the bold,
Together, let our truth unfold.

Crescendo of the Dreamers

In whispers soft, the dreams take flight,
They rise and swirl, a dance of light.
With hearts aflame, they chase the stars,
The pulse of hope, it heals the scars.

A symphony of thoughts and sighs,
In painted skies, ambition lies.
Together strong, they break the mold,
A tale of courage, waiting to unfold.

Each heartbeat hums, a rhythmic beat,
The journey's long, yet bittersweet.
Through shadows cast, they find their way,
In every dawn, they greet the day.

With voices raised, they spread their wings,
In unity, a chorus sings.
Boundless dreams, they intertwine,
A tapestry of hearts that shine.

So let us dance in twilight's gleam,
Together we rise, the age of dream.
With every note, our spirits soar,
In the crescendo, forevermore.

On the Wings of Purpose

On wings of purpose, we ascend,
Through valleys deep, our hearts extend.
With every breath, we find our way,
Embracing light that guides the day.

In visions clear, we seek the truth,
The strength within, the force of youth.
With steadfast resolve, we face the storm,
In unity, we draw our form.

Each step we take, a promise made,
In trials faced, our fears will fade.
Resilience blooms in darkest nights,
With every struggle, hope ignites.

Together we strive, with purpose bold,
In stories shared, our dreams unfold.
The path is bright with love and grace,
In every challenge, we find our place.

So here we stand, with open hearts,
On wings of purpose, we'll never part.
Through every trial, we will rise,
With faith as vast as endless skies.

Embracing the Infinite Sky

Beneath the heavens, dreams take flight,
They weave through clouds, embrace the night.
With every heartbeat, stars align,
In cosmic dance, our spirits shine.

The moonlight whispers, secrets true,
A canvas vast, painted anew.
With arms outstretched, we greet the dawn,
In every shadow, hope is drawn.

Through storms we travel, fierce and free,
In every heart, a melody.
The winds of change will guide our way,
As we unfold, a brighter day.

With courage held like wings of light,
Together, we face the endless night.
In unity, our voices blend,
Embracing all, our spirits mend.

So look above, the sky is wide,
With every dream, we turn the tide.
In infinite wonder, we will fly,
Forever free, embracing the sky.

The Ascent of Dreams Unfurling

With steady hearts, we climb the heights,
To grasp the dreams, to reach new sights.
Each step we take, a story told,
In every breath, our dreams unfold.

Through gentle winds, we seek the grace,
In every challenge, find our place.
The summit calls, a siren's song,
In the ascent, we all belong.

With hands entwined, we face the thrill,
In friendship forged, our dreams fulfill.
Together strong, we'll face the climb,
In every heartbeat, lost in rhyme.

As daylight breaks, the path shines clear,
In every hope, we conquer fear.
With open hearts, we rise and soar,
In unity, we are much more.

So let us dream beneath the stars,
In every moment, here we are.
With eyes alight, our spirits free,
The ascent, a song of destiny.

Beyond the Reach of Gravity

Weightless dreams drift in the night,
Floating softly, out of sight.
Stars whisper secrets, low and clear,
In this dance, we cast our fear.

Planets waltz in a cosmic game,
Galaxies sparkle, igniting flame.
Chasing shadows, we take our flight,
Beyond the bounds of day and night.

In this realm where spirits soar,
We find freedom, evermore.
Gravity's pull fades from view,
As we reach for what is true.

Infinite skies, an endless sea,
Unfolding paths, we long to be.
Bonded by dreams, we breathe in light,
Together in this endless night.

Enveloping the Clouds of Potential

Whispers of hope rise high above,
Carried softly on winds of love.
Clouds gather round, a canvas bright,
Each shape a dream, each hue a light.

Potential flows like rivers wide,
In hearts where aspirations reside.
Brush strokes of courage paint the sky,
A tapestry woven where spirits fly.

With each heartbeat, visions grow,
Seeds of promise, we plant and sow.
The horizon glows, an open door,
Inviting us to seek and soar.

The clouds embrace, no limits found,
In the heartbeat of the profound.
Together we dare to chase the dawn,
In the embrace of dreams reborn.

The Lightness of Reaching High

In the stillness, a whisper calls,
Gently urging us to rise and sprawl.
With wings of hope, we chart the sky,
In the lightness of dreams, we fly.

Each heartbeat lifts us, light as air,
A buoyant spirit, free from care.
The sun ignites our joyful flight,
Casting shadows, chasing light.

Clouds of doubt drift far away,
In the warmth of a brand new day.
Reaching high, we touch the sun,
In this dance, we are all one.

With every stride, we greet the stars,
Finding beauty, bound by scars.
Through the realms of endless sky,
In the lightness, we learn to fly.

Of Stars and Daring Hearts

Stars ignite the canvas vast,
In the night where shadows cast.
Daring hearts race through the dark,
Chasing dreams, they leave a mark.

Galaxies swirl in a cosmic ballet,
Guiding lost souls on their way.
Each twinkle a promise, every glance a sign,
In the universe, our hearts align.

Together we reach for the unknown,
Venturing paths where courage is grown.
With every step, the stars will cheer,
In this journey, we shed our fear.

Of daring hearts and endless skies,
We find the truth where freedom lies.
In the glow of those distant lights,
We become the dreamers of endless nights.

The Climb to Brilliance

Each step is forged with care,
Towards heights that none can spare.
The journey winds with trials bold,
Yet dreams ignite like fire in gold.

With every stumble, lessons call,
In shadows deep, we rise, we fall.
The summit gleams, a beacon bright,
For those who dare to chase the light.

Breathless winds whisper truth,
In the heart lies the fountain of youth.
Patience, strength, the road unspooled,
In perseverance, brilliance is fueled.

So up we go, through storm and strife,
Embracing the pulse of vibrant life.
For each ascent feeds the soul,
A journey where we learn to be whole.

A Symphony for the Soarers

From valleys low to heights unknown,
A symphony of dreams is sown.
With wings unfurled, we take our flight,
In harmony, we chase the night.

Each note a spark, each beat a guide,
We dance above, with hearts open wide.
Resounding echoes, tales of old,
In soaring rhythms, courage unfolds.

The winds carry our heartfelt song,
Uniting hearts where we belong.
We lift each other, spirits soar,
In this sweet symphony, we want more.

Together we shine, together we rise,
Our melodies touch the endless skies.
For every soarer knows their tune,
Is a celebration beneath the moon.

Into the Vast Unknown

Beyond the shores of what we know,
Lies a realm where wild dreams flow.
With open minds and spirits free,
We cross the waves of possibility.

Each hesitation, a whispered fear,
Yet courage guides us, crystal clear.
The stars above create our map,
As we navigate the cosmic gap.

Into the depths where wonders bloom,
Life bursts forth, dispelling gloom.
With every step, we uncover light,
In the vast unknown, we ignite.

Our hearts beat like a drum in tune,
With the rhythm of the universe in bloom.
For adventurers at heart, we roam,
Finding solace within the unknown.

Beyond the Echoes of Ordinary

In a world where colors blend,
We seek the lines that never end.
Beyond the echoes of routine's call,
Lies a place where dreams stand tall.

With every leap from common ground,
The extraordinary can be found.
In whispered secrets, the brave dare tread,
Where imagination weaves its thread.

The mundane fades beneath the sun,
As vibrant visions have begun.
Through valleys lush, and skies so wide,
We step away from time's keen tide.

In the embrace of what's unique,
The heart finds strength, the spirit speaks.
To dance beyond the ordinary glow,
Is to live where magic's seeds still grow.

Beyond the Fences of Doubt

In shadows cast by doubts and fears,
We find the strength to face our years.
With every step, the heart does soar,
Beyond the fences, there's so much more.

The whispers tell of dreams so bright,
Emerging from the endless night.
With courage wrapped around our soul,
We leap beyond, we reach our goal.

These tangled roots can bind us tight,
But we will push to find the light.
For every fall, we rise anew,
Beyond the fences, hopes break through.

The landscape shifts, horizons gleam,
We chase the whispers of our dream.
With every doubt cast far away,
We build our future day by day.

So let the world throw what it may,
We'll dance beneath the sun's warm ray.
Our spirits free, we're bold and proud,
Forever living, beyond the crowd.

A Serenade of Daring

In twilight hues, our voices blend,
A serenade, where spirits mend.
We summon dreams, we take our flight,
With hearts ablaze in endless night.

Through tangled woods, where shadows creep,
We find the path, though it is steep.
With every note, the courage grows,
A daring song the heart bestows.

The stars above, they wink and shine,
Guiding us towards a fate divine.
In rhythms bold, we carve our way,
In unity, we seize the day.

With every chord, a story told,
We break the chains, we dare be bold.
With voices strong, we'll pierce the veil,
A serenade, we will not fail.

So let the winds of fortune blow,
We'll plant our seeds, and watch them grow.
In daring steps, we chase the fire,
A melody that lifts us higher.

Manifesting the Beyond

Awake, arise, the dawn is near,
With minds aligned, we hold no fear.
The future calls, a siren's song,
We bend the will, to right the wrong.

In visions clear, our spirits gleam,
We chart the course, we chase the dream.
With every breath, we claim our space,
Beyond the bounds, we find our grace.

The canvas spread, our colors bright,
We'll paint the world with pure delight.
With open hearts, we stand as one,
Manifesting dreams beneath the sun.

Each moment rich with endless choice,
In silence, hear your inner voice.
Our hopes ignite, like stars above,
In unity, we rise in love.

Together now, we stake our claim,
In life's grand stage, we play our game.
The beyond awaits, let's venture wide,
In manifesting, we'll find our guide.

The Glimmer of Potential Heights

In whispers soft, potential glows,
A fire ignites, a fervent rose.
With every heartbeat, dreams take flight,
We seek the summits, pure delight.

The valleys low may hold us back,
But courage reigns, we'll stay on track.
In every challenge, lessons find,
A glimmer shines within the mind.

The paths we choose, they twist and turn,
With every step, our spirits burn.
As heights approach, we grow in grace,
Embracing change, we find our place.

In shared belief, we lift each other,
With open arms, we claim our tether.
The glimmer brightens, lighting skies,
Together soaring, we will rise.

So reach for stars that call your name,
In potential's dance, we stoke the flame.
With every breath, our dreams expand,
The heights we seek, together stand.

An Odyssey Through Aerial Dreams

In the sky where visions soar,
Colors blend, and spirits roar.
Whispers drift on clouds so light,
Guiding hearts through endless night.

Celestial paths of silver gleam,
Carving routes in the moon's beam.
Winds of change, they gently sway,
Leading us to a brighter day.

With every breath, we rise and ebb,
In the dance of life, we web.
Floating high, our worries cease,
Finding in the air, our peace.

Ode to dreams that take their flight,
Bathed in rays of morning light.
Boundless realms, our spirits chase,
Embracing time and endless space.

Each turn brings us closer still,
To the beat of heart and will.
Guided by the stars above,
We journey forth, forever in love.

Dancing with the Breezes of Desire

In twilight's glow, we find our grace,
The gentle winds, a soft embrace.
Whispers carried through the night,
Igniting dreams, igniting light.

Feet adorned with petals' hue,
We sway as one, the world anew.
Every twirl, a spark divine,
In the breeze, our hearts align.

Moonlit paths guide our way home,
In the stillness, we freely roam.
A symphony of breath and sighs,
Together, we'll touch the skies.

With desires woven in the air,
We spin, we laugh, beyond compare.
Each moment, a fleeting chance,
To lose ourselves in this sweet dance.

Time stands still, as we entwine,
A tapestry of souls that shine.
In the rhythm of the night,
We find our peace, our love, our light.

The Rise of Unyielding Spirits

Through mountains high and valleys low,
A spirit fierce begins to grow.
With every trial faced anew,
Resilience forged, our strength breaks through.

Voices echo through the storm,
Each heartbeat sets a brand new norm.
Determined souls with fire ignite,
Transforming darkness into light.

A chorus rises, bold and true,
Carving paths, we break right through.
Hand in hand, we share the weight,
Together we defy our fate.

From ashes, we shall rise again,
Through struggles faced, we shall gain.
With courage born in every scar,
We paint the skies, our spirits star.

In unity, we'll stand so tall,
Echoing the strength of all.
With hearts ablaze, we'll fight the night,
Boundlessly reaching for the light.

Sketching Dreams in the Air

With gentle strokes, we trace the sky,
As dreams take shape, we learn to fly.
Each canvas brushed by hopes anew,
Imagination blooms, bright and true.

In the azure, colors blend,
Crafting visions, we ascend.
With every thought, a picture spins,
A masterpiece where life begins.

Whirling thoughts in endless flight,
Ink of stars, we sketch the night.
Dreams unfurl with every breath,
Creating life that conquers death.

From whispers soft to vibrant hues,
Our hearts embrace these vibrant views.
In fantasies, we find our home,
Exploring realms where we can roam.

So let us paint, let us declare,
The beauty found in open air.
For dreams, once sketched, will always stay,
In the heart's canvas, come what may.

Harnessing the Cosmic Currents

In the silence of the night, we soar,
Stitching dreams to the stars we implore.
With every breath, we feel the tides,
A dance of fate where wonder abides.

Mysteries woven in silver streams,
Galaxies whisper our secret dreams.
Chasing shadows, we sail afar,
Guided gently by a distant star.

Each moment flows like a river wide,
Connecting us all, our timeless guide.
Light years apart, yet close in heart,
Together we'll craft our cosmic art.

Harnessing winds from realms unknown,
We'll chart a course to worlds unshown.
With hope as our compass, and love as our aim,
We'll rise to the heights, embracing the flame.

As the universe swirls in a cosmic dance,
We'll seize the magic, take every chance.
For in this journey, so vast and grand,
We'll write our story, hand in hand.

The Beacon Beyond the Horizon

A flicker of light calls out to the sea,
It dances on waves, inviting me.
Towards the sunrise, where dreams are born,
I set my course, feeling hope's adorn.

The horizon stretches, an endless embrace,
A promise of journeys, a wild chase.
Each heartbeat echoes, a lullaby sweet,
Guiding me forward, this path I will greet.

In the mist of the morning, I hear a song,
A melody tender, where I belong.
It speaks of courage, of battles fought,
A beacon of strength, a lesson sought.

As clouds drift softly, and shadows shift,
I gather the light, let my spirit lift.
For beyond the horizon, where dreams collide,
Awaits a tomorrow, where hope won't hide.

With each step taken, I savor the view,
The world unfolds, rich in every hue.
A journey of hearts, where we'll ignite,
The beacon beyond, our guiding light.

A Heart with No Limits

In the expanse where emotions run free,
There lies a heart, wild as the sea.
With every beat, it yearns to explore,
Beyond the confines, forever to soar.

Beneath the surface, love's currents flow,
A river of passion, eager to grow.
No chains can bind what the soul believes,
For a heart unshackled, no one deceives.

It laughs with the stars, it dances with light,
Unraveled by dreams that take flight at night.
A unity woven, where courage ignites,
The fire within, a series of flights.

In valleys of shadows, it stands so bold,
Filled with the warmth of stories untold.
A heart with no limits, no bounds to its grace,
In the vastness of life, it finds its own place.

So listen closely, let your spirit unwind,
For in every heartbeat, true freedom you'll find.
Let the rhythm guide you, no fear to incite,
A heart with no limits will conquer the night.

The Quest for the Infinite Blue

In the realm of dreams, we take to the sky,
Chasing horizons where hopes never die.
With each step forward, the world opens wide,
A canvas of azure, where visions collide.

Whispers of oceans, calling us near,
The depths of our souls dance without fear.
We search for the treasure that lies out of view,
In the quest for the endless, the infinite blue.

Every wave carries secrets, beckoning we,
To venture to places where hearts can be free.
With the wind at our backs and the sun in our gaze,
We'll ride through the storms, the wild and the haze.

Through valleys of twilight, we'll wander and roam,
In pursuit of our dreams, we'll create a new home.
The echoes of laughter will guide us anew,
In the quest for forever, the infinite blue.

As the stars twinkle soft in the deep velvet night,
We'll raise our voices, basking in light.
For the journey we take is the treasure we seek,
In the infinite blue, we find what is unique.

A Journey Beyond the Clouds

Above the mist where dreams take flight,
A voyage starts in morning light.
With every step, new lands to see,
A world awaits, wild and free.

Mountains gleam with silver hue,
The sky adorned in shades of blue.
Each whisper of the winds we heed,
As heart and soul begin to lead.

Through valleys deep and rivers wide,
With courage found, we push aside.
The fears that once held tight their grip,
We'll sail on hope, a steady ship.

In twilight's glow, the path revealed,
Our hearts awake, each dream is sealed.
In unity, we face the night,
Together bound in shared delight.

Beyond the clouds, our spirits soar,
In every heartbeat, we explore.
For life's a journey, rich and vast,
In every moment, hold it fast.

Navigating the Winds of Hope

In gentle breezes, whispers call,
They guide us forward, through it all.
With sails unfurled and hearts that trust,
We ride the winds, as dreams combust.

Each breeze a promise, soft and kind,
The path ahead begins to unwind.
With every gust, a choice we face,
To find our rhythm, to find our place.

Through tempest's roar and skies of gray,
Hope shines a light to lead the way.
In moments still, we hear it clear,
The winds of change are drawing near.

With courage bold, we chart the course,
Embracing all—in joy, in force.
The world is vast, with roads untried,
In winds of hope, our hearts abide.

So let the currents fill our sails,
Across the vast, where courage prevails.
Together we rise, we will not cease,
Navigating toward our sweet release.

Lifted by the Zephyr

A gentle touch, the zephyr's song,
It lifts us high where we belong.
With open hearts and wings outspread,
We dance through air, where dreams are bred.

In softest whispers, secrets glide,
Through swaying trees and rivers wide.
The breezes carry tales of old,
In every gust, new hopes are bold.

With every breath, the world anew,
The past behind, the future's view.
Against the storms, we rise and sway,
Lifted by winds, we find our way.

As sunbeams kiss the hills afire,
We follow paths that never tire.
In zephyr's arms, we grow and change,
The beauty found in every range.

Together soaring through the skies,
We reach for dreams that never die.
In each soft breeze, our spirits free,
The zephyr sings: just come with me.

Echoes of the Unseen Heights

Soft echoes linger in the air,
Of heights unseen, beyond compare.
They call to souls who long to rise,
To chase the stars, to touch the skies.

In whispers low, the mountains speak,
Of journeys long and visions peak.
With every step, we heed the call,
In unity, we rise or fall.

To climb the cliffs of doubt and fear,
With every echo, courage near.
Through shadows cast and light that beams,
We find the power in our dreams.

For heights unseen bring forth the fight,
To turn the dark into the light.
With every breath, our voices blend,
In echoes sweet that never end.

So let the call of heights inspire,
Our dreams aflame, our hearts afire.
Together bound, we'll reach the skies,
In echoes warm, our spirits rise.

A Dance with the Wild Skies

In whispers, clouds drift high,
The sun spills gold on wings,
We twirl with the breezy sigh,
In freedom, our spirit sings.

Stars collide in cosmic play,
Moonlight bathes the earth below,
In night's embrace, we'll sway,
As time, like rivers, flows.

With every gust that swells,
We chase the untamed light,
In nature's pulse, love dwells,
Together, hearts take flight.

Echoes of thunder throng,
As shadows waltz with grace,
In storms, we find our song,
As wildness we embrace.

Our hearts like kites are free,
Tethered to the sky's blue,
In this wild symphony,
The dance is just for two.

Boundless Aspirations

Reaching heights that kiss the sun,
We chase dreams bold and bright,
With every heartbeat, we run,
Boundless hopes ignite.

The horizon calls our names,
With whispers soft and clear,
In the pursuit of our flames,
We shed every fear.

Mountains rise, a challenge fierce,
Yet we stand undeterred,
The strength within us, a fierce force,
In passion, we are stirred.

With open minds, we explore,
The paths less traveled wide,
Each step we take, we soar,
With visions as our guide.

Together we will climb,
To peaks that reach the sky,
In this dance of time,
Our spirits will not die.

The Summit Beckons

The summit waits, a silent throne,
Veiled in mist and dreams,
Bold hearts venture forth alone,
Through nature's wild schemes.

With every step, the air grows thin,
But resolve lights our way,
The journey's worth, the fire within,
To greet the breaking day.

We climb where eagles dare to soar,
On trails of rock and stone,
With hands that scrape, we seek for more,
For heights we can call our own.

The summit whispers sweetly now,
Of triumph and release,
As we make a solemn vow,
In unity, find peace.

Together we will plant our flag,
And claim the sky's embrace,
With every sweat, no room for lag,
In victory's warm grace.

Embracing the Aether

In the realm where dreams reside,
We wander, hand in hand,
Through the currents, we will glide,
In this ethereal land.

With whispers of the cosmic flow,
We dance among the stars,
In the magic of the glow,
We leave behind our scars.

The aether calls our souls to play,
With colors yet unseen,
In the light of a new day,
We paint the skies so green.

Floating on a gentle breeze,
We let go of our chains,
In the stillness, peace can tease,
As love's sweet song remains.

Together we are boundless, true,
In realms beyond the sight,
In the vastness, me and you,
We'll chase the endless light.

The Soar of Determination

With wings of grit, I rise each day,
Facing storms that come my way.
Climbing peaks, I won't retreat,
In every challenge, I find my beat.

The skies are vast, my spirit free,
I chase the dreams that call to me.
Through trials faced, and fears I've known,
I've found the strength to stand alone.

Each heartbeat sings a battle's song,
In the depths, where I belong.
With every step, I carve my path,
Through shadows long, I face the wrath.

The flame within will never dim,
With every fall, I rise again.
A heart that beats for what is true,
Awakens fire, a light anew.

I soar above, my spirit flies,
For in my heart, the courage lies.
With hope as fuel, I'll chart the skies,
And seek the sun, where freedom lies.

Fluttering towards Tomorrow

On gentle winds, I spread my wings,
In search of joy, the future brings.
With every flutter, hopes take flight,
To dance with dreams beneath the light.

The dawn unfolds with colors bright,
I chase the warmth, embracing light.
With every breath, I find my song,
In this journey, I belong.

Though clouds may gather, dark and grey,
I'll keep on soaring, come what may.
The horizon calls with whispers sweet,
A promise waits where air and earth meet.

With open heart, I face the day,
To find the bliss that guides my way.
And as the stars light up the night,
I'll follow dreams that feel so right.

So here I am, a soul in flight,
Toward tomorrow, bold and bright.
With every moment that I earn,
I flutter forth, for hope's return.

Chasing the Sunlight

With every dawn, I chase the light,
From shadows deep to skies so bright.
I hold my dreams within my hands,
To journey forth across the lands.

The golden rays, a guiding call,
I rise and shine, refuse to fall.
Through valleys low and mountains steep,
The sun will lead where courage leaps.

In countless hues, the day unfolds,
A tapestry of tales retold.
Each moment glows with vibrant grace,
Inviting me to find my place.

Though night may come with whispered fears,
I'll light the way with hopeful tears.
For in the dark, the stars emerge,
To lift my heart, to surge and urge.

So here I stand, unyielding bright,
Chasing dreams, embracing light.
With the sun above, I dare to run,
For every journey has begun.

Echoes of a Higher Calling

In silence deep, a voice resounds,
With gentle whispers, truth abounds.
It calls my spirit to the sky,
To seek the stars, to learn to fly.

Across the hills and valleys wide,
I follow where the dreams reside.
Each step I take, a path unfolds,
In echoes rich, my heart consoled.

The winds of change begin to blow,
They carry seeds of things to grow.
With open arms, I greet the new,
For in my heart, I know what's true.

The light above will guide my way,
Through darkest nights, to brighter days.
With every echo, strength I gain,
I rise above the doubt and pain.

In this symphony of the divine,
I find my purpose to align.
For in the depths of my own being,
Are echoes clear, forever freeing.

The Burgeoning of New Horizons

In twilight's glow, dreams start to bloom,
A whisper of dawn joins night's gentle gloom.
Each hope takes flight, on wings made of light,
As stars watch in awe, the canvas ignites.

Through valleys deep, where shadows once lay,
The heart stirs with grace, it knows not delay.
New paths emerge, like rivers that flow,
Embracing the change, we watch nature grow.

Mountains stand tall, yet can't block the sun,
For each step we take, new journeys begun.
With courage, we rise, like suns in the sky,
A chorus of voices, our spirits fly high.

The breeze carries tales of the brave and bold,
In the tapestry woven, new stories unfold.
With every heartbeat, let purpose align,
Together we soar, as the stars brightly shine.

In the warmth of the dawn, our vision takes shape,
A world redefined, by dreams we drape.
We cherish this moment, a gift from above,
As our hearts intertwine in the dance of love.

Unraveling Potential

Within each soul, a spark softly resides,
A map made of dreams where passion abides.
The layers of doubt are slowly revealed,
As light seeps through cracks, our fate is sealed.

Brick by brick, we dismantle the wall,
With whispers of courage, we answer the call.
Each breath a chance, each thought a relay,
In the game of life, we find our own way.

With every misstep, new lessons arise,
The heart learns to break, then learns how to rise.
With the winds of change, our vision expands,
Creating a future where purpose commands.

As rivers twist, so too does our fate,
Beneath all the layers, we find what's innate.
Through trials and joys, the truth will unveil,
The depth of our dreams will always prevail.

So trust in the journey; it's yours to unfold,
With threads of ambition, weave stories bold.
Our spirits ignite with the fire we share,
Together we rise, as we dare to care.

The Flutter of Unstoppable Intent

In the still of the night, intentions take flight,
With whispers of passion, they dance with delight.
Like feathers they glide, soft yet profound,
Each heartbeat a promise, a vow unbound.

Waves crash and roar, but we find our calm,
In the storm of our dreams, we grow and we qualm.
The pulse of our hopes beats strong in the haze,
While visions of future ignite our gaze.

With the dawn's first light, potential ignites,
Unstoppable force, as destiny writes.
Each flutter a step, each movement a cheer,
Embracing the power, we cast off our fear.

The art of intention, a beautiful play,
In the symphony of life, we find our own way.
Together we soar, relentless, unbound,
In the dance of existence, our truth shall resound.

With each silent wish, the universe bends,
Our spirits conjoin as true magic ascends.
In the flutter of dreams, our essence shines bright,
Unstoppable intent, as we chase the light.

Carving Trails in the Sky

In the canvas above, our dreams intertwine,
With strokes of ambition, our hearts align.
Each comet that passes, a wish on the rise,
We're sculpting our futures in vast open skies.

With kite strings of hope, we're ready to soar,
Chasing horizons we've yet to explore.
The winds of adventure whisper and tease,
As we carve out the trails that dance with the breeze.

From peaks to the valleys, our journey unfolds,
In the library of skies, each color retold.
With laughter and dreams, we paint our own tale,
A map made of courage, where we cannot fail.

As stars serve as guides, and clouds shift and sway,
We trust in each moment, come what may.
The echoes of freedom sing loud and clear,
In the sky's vast embrace, we conquer our fear.

So let's draw our paths in the great azure sea,
With hearts that are open and minds that are free.
As we carve our own trails through the heavens so high,
Together, forever, we'll soar through the sky.

The Pathway to the Stars

In the silence of the night,
Whispers of dreams take flight.
Guiding hearts through the dark,
Each step a shimmering spark.

Stars above, they twinkle bright,
Lighting up our hopeful sight.
With every wish we dare to make,
The cosmos trembles, stirs awake.

Galaxies swirl in the vast expanse,
Inviting us to take a chance.
Hand in hand, we wander far,
Discovering who we truly are.

Beyond the veil of earthly care,
The universe invites to dare.
We follow trails of milky light,
Onward, upward, into the night.

With each breath, we inhale grace,
In this eternal, boundless space.
Together we traverse the skies,
Awakening the heart's true rise.

Elevation of the Heart

Amidst the storms, we find our calm,
With every beat, a healing balm.
Through trials faced, our spirits rise,
Love's embrace, where hope lies.

In a world of rush and noise,
We seek the peace that brings us joys.
Through gentle whispers, we take flight,
Elevated by love's pure light.

Every challenge, a chance to grow,
With open hearts, we let it flow.
The power of love, our guiding star,
Transforms our wounds, no matter how far.

As the sun sets and the moon glows,
We only follow where the heart knows.
Upward we move, shedding our fears,
Moments cherished throughout the years.

In the tapestry of life we weave,
Every thread, a gift we receive.
Elevation is found in each part,
As we soar on the wings of the heart.

The Unfolding of Endless Horizons

Beyond the mountains, valleys wide,
Awaits a journey, a wondrous ride.
With every sunrise, hopes ignite,
An unfolding path, future in sight.

Step by step, with courage anew,
We chase the dreams that feel so true.
Every moment, a chance to see,
Horizons stretching, wild and free.

In the dance of clouds, we find our place,
Embracing life with an open grace.
Waves of time, they guide and sway,
To horizons bright, we find our way.

With open hearts and kindness shared,
Navigating paths that few have dared.
The world unfolds, as dreams collide,
In unity, we rise, no need to hide.

Together we breathe, as one we roam,
Finding beauty in every home.
For in this life, we all belong,
To horizons vast, where we are strong.

From Roots to Radiance

Deep in the earth, our roots entwine,
Drawing strength from the life divine.
With every season, we trace our line,
Transforming shadows into shine.

Through storms and trials, we learn to stand,
Nature's quiet, guiding hand.
With every rise, we touch the sky,
Embracing the gifts that life supply.

In the growth, we find our voice,
From humble soil, we make our choice.
To break the ground and seek the sun,
In unity, we are never done.

With colors bright, we paint the day,
Radiance found in every way.
The journey blooms, the heart expands,
From roots to heights, where love commands.

As we flourish, we share our light,
Illuminating the darkest night.
From roots to radiance, we embrace,
The beauty of life, our sacred space.

Transcending the Boundaries of Earth

We gaze upon the distant sky,
As whispers of the stars fly high.
Each heartbeat echoes tales of yore,
A longing for what lies in store.

With wings of light we dare to soar,
Across each horizon we explore.
The mountains bow, the rivers flow,
In unity, our dreams now grow.

From valleys deep to peaks so tall,
We chase the shadows, heed the call.
Beyond the limits set by fate,
In wonder, we will navigate.

The earth may bind, but hearts are free,
To seek what's known, yet yet to be.
For every step on sacred ground,
Brings forth a future yet unbound.

Transcending realms of time and space,
We carve our paths with love and grace.
In every pulse, the universe,
A cosmic dance, a timeless verse.

The Fabric of Elevated Dreams

In twilight's glow, our visions blend,
With threads of hope, we seek to mend.
Each stitch a wish, each knot a goal,
We weave our stories, heart and soul.

The clouds above, like cotton spun,
In sunlight's kiss, our journey's begun.
We float on dreams, aloft, sublime,
In every breath, we dance through time.

Illusions of the night unfold,
In patterns bright, our tales retold.
With every heartbeat, we ascend,
To realms where fears begin to bend.

The fabric holds our hopes so dear,
In woven threads, we cast out fear.
From depths below to mountains high,
We soar in colors, free and spry.

The tapestry of life and light,
In unity, we shine so bright.
Together we design our dreams,
In woven worlds, we find our themes.

In Pursuit of Celestial Realms

We chase the stars, a whispered quest,
In twilight's arms, our hearts find rest.
Amongst the moons, we seek the light,
To bridge the day with endless night.

The skies unfold a mystic map,
A cosmic dance, a gentle clap.
We wander far through galaxy's seam,
In pursuit of each ethereal dream.

With every step, the cosmos spins,
As echoes hum what joy begins.
Through rifts in space, our visions fly,
In pursuit of wonders up high.

With stars as guides, we find our way,
Past nebulae where shadows play.
In whispers soft, the heavens sing,
Of mysteries and the hope they bring.

In realms unbound, we seek to be,
With open hearts, we dare to dream.
Our spirits rise, eclipsing space,
In pursuit of a boundless grace.

Charting Paths of Distinction

On roads less traveled, we embark,
With courage bright, we leave our mark.
Each step a verse, each turn a rhyme,
In life's grand book, we write our time.

With compass set on dreams that gleam,
We traverse realms where few have seen.
In every choice, distinction grows,
Through trials faced, our courage shows.

The maps we draw are not of old,
But paths of wisdom, paths of gold.
With every journey, lessons learned,
In every turn, new visions burned.

Together bound, we chart the night,
In unity, our spirits light.
For every dream that we pursue,
A legacy of love rings true.

By forging trails in skies so vast,
We honor both the future and past.
In paths of distinction, we will find,
The harmony of heart and mind.

The Odyssey of the Untamed Spirit

In the wild where whispers roam,
A spirit dances, far from home.
Through valleys deep and mountains high,
An echo of freedom, a birdsong's cry.

Beneath the stars, dreams take flight,
Challenging shadows, embracing the night.
With every step, a tale unfolds,
In the heart of the brave, a fire bold.

Journeying forth, unchained and free,
The untamed spirit dares to be.
Through storms that rage and skies that weep,
Its roar rises, through the dark, it leaps.

Across the seas, where wild winds play,
It sails uncharted, come what may.
With passion as compass, heart as guide,
Onward it surges, with untamed pride.

In every struggle, wisdom seeds,
The spirit thrives, in love it feeds.
A journey long, yet it won't cease,
For every trial births sweet release.

Riding the Currents of Possibility

On shimmering waves, a vision gleams,
Where hopes collide and whisper dreams.
With sails unfurled, the winds do call,
To ride the currents, to brave the fall.

With every breath, new chances rise,
Painting colors in the skies.
Each moment, a chance to redefine,
The path we choose, the stars align.

Through turbulent waters, we dance and sway,
Embracing the changes, come what may.
The rhythm of life, a symphony grand,
Together we journey, hand in hand.

From valleys low to peaks so high,
We seek the truth, we do not shy.
With courage as anchor, faith as sail,
We'll navigate dreams, we shall not fail.

For every wave that crashes near,
Brings forth the strength to persevere.
With hearts wide open, we'll seize the day,
Riding the currents, come what may.

Owning the Open Sky

With arms outstretched, we greet the dawn,
In the vast expanse, our fears are gone.
Skyward we soar, like birds in flight,
Claiming our dreams in the morning light.

The clouds our canvas, painted bright,
Whispers of freedom ignite our flight.
A tapestry woven with colors bold,
In the heart's chamber, our stories told.

Each gust of wind, a gentle friend,
With every heartbeat, we ascend.
No chains can bind, no walls confine,
In the open sky, our spirits shine.

From peaks of ambition, we gaze below,
Embracing the vastness, letting go.
In this space, we find our peace,
Owning the sky, our sweet release.

With every sunset, the colors blend,
We conquer fears, we will not bend.
The horizon calls, our journey unfurls,
Owning the open sky, we own the worlds.

The Electrical Charge of Desire

In shadows deep, a spark ignites,
A current flows, illuminating nights.
With every pulse, the heart does race,
Desire's dance, an electrifying chase.

Through whispered dreams and secret sighs,
The voltage rises, the spirit flies.
In passion's grip, we lose control,
Electric waves consume the soul.

In midnight hours, our silence screams,
Awakening truths buried in dreams.
Fractured moments, a thrilling tease,
The charge of desire, an endless breeze.

Through storms of longing, we often tread,
In currents of chaos, we are led.
With each spark igniting the night,
The dance of desire, a magnetic flight.

Unraveled hearts, where energies blend,
In this electric field, there is no end.
With every heartbeat, a powerful force,
The charge of desire, our soul's true course.

Flights of Unspoken Dreams

In the hush of twilight skies,
Whispers glide on silver wings.
Fragrant hopes begin to rise,
While the heart softly sings.

Stars awake to paint the night,
Guiding visions, bold and bright.
Each desire, a hidden light,
Drawing paths to endless flight.

Clouds cradle the thoughts we share,
As they drift through midnight air.
Chasing shadows, without care,
Fleeting moments, rare and fair.

Graceful journeys yet to take,
Beneath the moon's soft embrace.
With each step, we dare to wake,
Unravel dreams time can't erase.

So we follow where they lead,
Unfolding layers of our soul.
In the silence, hearts take heed,
And unspoken dreams make whole.

Charting Celestial Courses

Beneath the vast cosmic sea,
Stars align in radiant streams.
Navigators wild and free,
Charting paths through woven dreams.

Asteroids whisper ancient lore,
While comets blaze with desire.
Galaxies beckon us to soar,
From earthbound thoughts, we aspire.

In the dark, we find our way,
Guided by celestial signs.
Each spark brings a brand new day,
Whispering of love divine.

Endless vastness fuels the quest,
For the heart leaps at the chance.
Across the stars, we are blessed,
In this cosmic, wondrous dance.

Destinies woven with delight,
In the tapestry of night.
We take flight, hearts ever bright,
Boundless dreams within our sight.

Elevate Your Spirit

In the calm of morning light,
Find your breath, let it flow.
Lift your gaze, embrace the height,
Where the hopeful spirits go.

With each step upon the ground,
Leave behind your silent fears.
In the beauty, joy is found,
In the laughter and the tears.

Let the music fill your soul,
Dance with winds that lift you high.
Radiate and become whole,
Chasing dreams that touch the sky.

Every moment is a gift,
Let it shine and quench your thirst.
Feel the energy, the lift,
In this life, we are immersed.

So rise up and take your flight,
On the wings of love and grace.
Elevate through day and night,
In each heart, a sacred space.

The Drive to Touch the Sun

With a heart ablaze and bold,
We chase the horizon's gleam.
Fingers stretch to grasp the gold,
Driven by an endless dream.

Stories written in the skies,
Every moment a new spark.
Fueled by passion, truth, and sighs,
We venture forth into the dark.

No limits bound the soul's ascent,
As we dance on solar rays.
A fire within, a mind unbent,
Igniting dreams in bright displays.

Through tempest winds and night's embrace,
We carry on, with love as guide.
Facing each challenge we must face,
In the struggle, joy and pride.

The sun awaits with arms so wide,
For those who dare to seek its light.
With every heartbeat, hearts collide,
And together, we rise in flight.

The Zephyr of Hope

A whisper soft through the trees,
Carries dreams on a gentle breeze.
In twilight's blush, shadows play,
Embers glow as night turns to day.

With each dawn, a promise reborn,
Tales of joy and hearts in sworn.
Through storms we walk, hand in hand,
Together we rise, together we stand.

The zephyr sings of brighter skies,
In the depths, hope never dies.
It lifts us high, beyond the fray,
Guiding our path, lighting the way.

In quiet moments, we find our peace,
Where worries fade, and troubles cease.
Embracing the dawn, our spirits soar,
For hope endures, forevermore.

Flight Paths of the Heart

Like swallows dance in the summer air,
Our hearts take flight without a care.
Through valleys low and mountains high,
We chase the stars across the sky.

In laughter shared, in silent tears,
We build our dreams through all our years.
With every heartbeat, we chart our course,
Navigating love's unyielding force.

The winds may shift, the skies may darken,
Yet in our souls, the light will hearken.
Together we rise, forever free,
In the dance of love, just you and me.

So let us soar on wings of trust,
In every flight, in every gust.
For paths we take are ours alone,
In every heart, a home is grown.

Navigating the Currents of Desire

In the river's flow, our passions blend,
With gentle bends that never end.
Each ripple sings a tune so sweet,
Mapping our dreams where souls do meet.

The currents surge with wild delight,
Leading us on through day and night.
In whispered words, our wishes cast,
We'll brave the storms, our love steadfast.

With every tide, our hopes arise,
Reflecting deep beneath the skies.
For in the depths, where shadows hide,
We find the truth that love provides.

So let us sail with hearts ablaze,
Through roughest seas and sunlit days.
In each embrace, desire flows,
Together we chart how passion grows.

The Altitude of Resolve

From peaks of strength, we gain our view,
With steadfast hearts and courage true.
Through every trial, we climb anew,
Embracing heights, we push on through.

In valleys low, where shadows loom,
Our spirits rise, dispelling gloom.
With every step, our dreams align,
In the altitude where hopes entwine.

The air grows thin, but fears will cease,
In unity, we find our peace.
Through every leap, through every fall,
We gather strength, we give our all.

So here we stand, on mountains high,
With hearts ablaze, we touch the sky.
In the altitude of dreams fulfilled,
Together we rise, together we build.